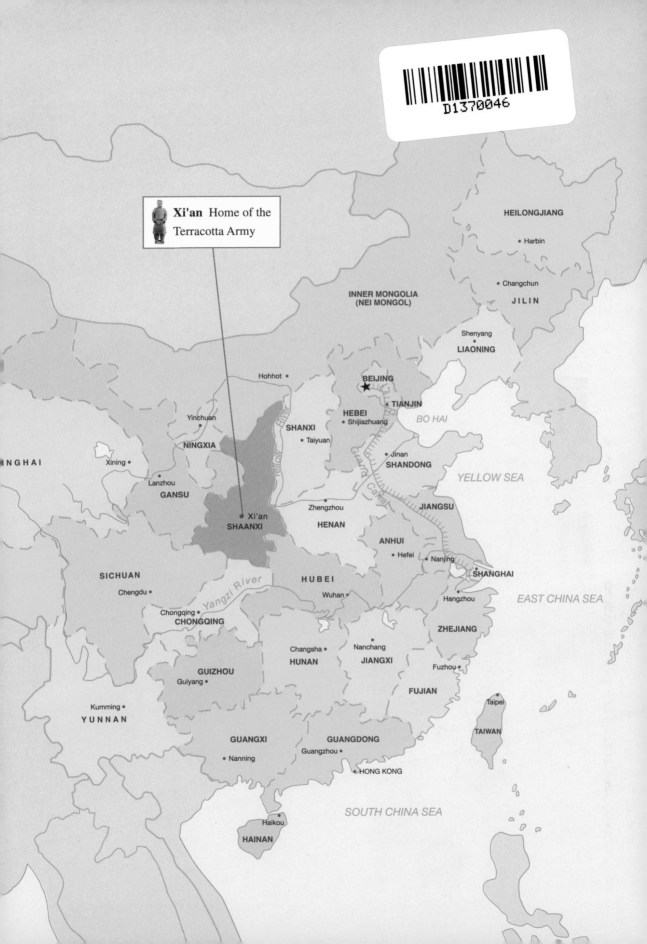

Xi'an Home of the Terracotta Army

HEILONGJIANG

• Harbin

• Changchun

JILIN

INNER MONGOLIA
(NEI MONGOL)

Shenyang •
LIAONING

Hohhot •

BEIJING
★

• TIANJIN

Yinchuan •

SHANXI

HEBEI
• Shijiazhuang

BO HAI

NINGXIA

• Taiyuan

NGHAI

Xining •

• Jinan
SHANDONG

YELLOW SEA

Lanzhou •
GANSU

Zhengzhou •

JIANGSU

Xi'an •
SHAANXI

HENAN

ANHUI

• Hefei

• Nanjing

SICHUAN

HUBEI

SHANGHAI

Chengdu •

Wuhan •

Hangzhou •

EAST CHINA SEA

Chongqing •
CHONGQING

Yangzi River

ZHEJIANG

Changsha •

Nanchang •

GUIZHOU

HUNAN

JIANGXI

Fuzhou •

Guiyang •

FUJIAN

Kumming •
YUNNAN

Taipei •

GUANGXI

GUANGDONG

TAIWAN

• Nanning

Guangzhou •

• HONG KONG

SOUTH CHINA SEA

Haikou •
HAINAN

THE TERRACOTTA ARMY

OF THE FIRST EMPEROR OF CHINA

THE TERRACOTTA ARMY OF THE FIRST EMPEROR OF CHINA

The buried army of the First Emperor of China is one of the largest and most stunning archaeological finds of the 20th century. Discovered in 1974 at Lintong, 35 kilometres east of Xi'an, the warriors and horses have deservedly become known as a Wonder of the World. Now exhibited *in situ*, the life-size terracotta figures so far excavated testify to the power of the man for whom they were moulded to protect in afterlife — Emperor Qin Shihuangdi, the First Emperor of China (259-210BC).

The Rise of Qin

At the sight of the massed ranks of these warriors and horses one is naturally prompted by their number and magnificence to ask questions about Qin Shihuangdi. Who was he? How did he become emperor of the first unified empire of China? And what kind of policies did he enact to control his vast territory?

More than 2,400 years ago, the political map of China resembled a jigsaw. At least 12 kingdoms existed, spread across northern, central and eastern China as we know it today. These kingdoms were in a constant state of war, hence this period is now referred to as the Warring States era (475-221BC). One of the most powerful states was Qin, which held sway over the middle reaches of the Yellow River, specifically much of present-day Shaanxi, southeast Gansu, northern Sichuan and the Ningxia Hui Autonomous Region.

(Preceding page) An archer, 1.87 metres in height, standing at ease. Excavated from Pit Number One, this warrior once held a bow in his right hand. Most weapons were looted by tomb robbers when Xiang Yu's peasant army ransacked the Qin mausoleum. (Top right) Face of a general exhibiting racial characteristics common to the whole army: a squarish face, thick lips and facial hair in the form of a beard. (Bottom) Army formation in Pit Number One showing the columns of warriors behind the vanguard.

The parentage of Qin Shihuangdi (who was named Ying Zheng) is something of an enigma. His father Zichu, a son of the King of Qin, was sent as hostage to the Zhao State during a dispute between the neighbouring kingdoms. The young hostage, apparently allowed to live relatively freely in Zhao, became acquainted with a prosperous and conniving merchant named Lü Buwei. Lü Buwei had a favourite concubine, a dancer. When the hostage became infatuated with her, Lü Buwei not only stepped aside, but even helped him and the concubine to escape to Qin, where Zichu eventually became king. Shortly after their arrival in Qin, Ying Zheng was born to the dancer, but whether his natural father was Zichu, or Lü Buwei, has kept historians perplexed ever since.

Ascending the throne when he was only 13 years old, Ying Zheng appointed Lü Buwei as his counsellor, and thus the cunning ex-merchant effectively controlled the kingdom of Qin for a decade until he was finally banished and replaced by another adviser, Li Si.

(Top) Rubbing from a stele, exhibited in Xi'an's Shaanxi Museum, depicting an image of Emperor Qin Shihuangdi. (Bottom) A seated horse groom, 68 cm in height, excavated from a horse grave within the Qin mausoleum. (Following page) A commander in armour, 1.90 metres in height, excavated from Pit Number One. He once held weapons in both hands: a spear in his right hand, but the strange twisted position of his left hand remains a mystery and the weapon he once held in it is unknown.

With the ministerial talents of Li Si, complemented by the military capabilities of the officer Meng Tian, Qin grew more prosperous and increased its offensives against the rival kingdoms. By 221BC the remaining six main kingdoms — Han, Zhao, Wei, Chu, Yan and Qi — had been conquered and assimilated. Ying Zheng had acted with as much swiftness and determination as a 'silkworm devouring a mulberry leaf', in the words of the historian Sima Qian. The entire territory of what was then China had been united under him, and the first centralized empire had been established. It stretched from the east China coast to Lintao in the west, and from the Lang Mountains to the Yalu River in the north. A tongue of territory even extended south into present-day Vietnam.

Ancient legends told of three saintly sovereigns, *huang*, and five ideal emperors, *di*. To reflect his supreme achievements and the unprecedented extent of his rule, Ying Zheng adopted the title *huangdi* ; this was prefixed by Qin, the name of his 'native' state, and *shi*, meaning the first. His full title thus proclaimed the establishment of an empire and dynasty.

To consolidate his power, Qin Shihuangdi embarked on a vast reform programme

(Top) Ming Great Wall. Wall-building, adopted by Qin Shihuangdi as a means of defending the northern flank of the empire, was continued as a national defence strategy by many emperors in Chinese history.

encompassing military, political, social and administrative matters. Inter-kingdom defensive walls, which stood in the way of centralization, were destroyed, but those of the former Zhao and Yan kingdoms in the north were utilized by General Meng Tian in building what was the first Great Wall. This barrier, stretching approximately 2,500 kilometres from Lintao, south of Lanzhou in the west, to the Yalu River in the northeast, shielded the Qin empire from attacks by nomads of the north.

Not all changes were on such a gargantuan scale. One peculiar reform standardized the axle lengths on carts to two metres to ease their passage along the wheel ruts of the ever-increasing number of roads which radiated from the capital Xianyang (25 kilometres west of today's Xi'an) to all parts of the empire. These arteries guaranteed the swift deployment of the army to put down rebellions. To the same end, metal weapons were confiscated and taken to Xianyang where they were melted down. Legend has it that they were recast into 12 giant statues which lined the approach to the

imperial palace.

Weights, measures and coinage were also standardized to strengthen commerce. In the Warring States period, the contending kingdoms had their own coinage, but now only the Qin form — a round coin with a hole in the middle — was circulated. The written language, which had regional differences, was unified by the banning of old character forms and the compulsory adoption of the *xiaozhuan* and *lishu* scripts. Tens of thousands of the empire's richest and most powerful families were brought by force to live in the capital where they could be kept under observation.

The emperor's attempts to maintain a grasp on order went further. He divided his empire into 36 new administrative districts and posted garrisons at the most strategic locations. During the five inspection tours of his domain that he made during his rule, political propaganda was used to

(Top) Earthen ramparts of the Qin Kingdom (one of the Warring States) defensive wall (c. 287BC), later strengthened and incorporated into the line of the first Great Wall, constructed during Qin Dynasty times around 214BC. (Left) Qin coin, with characters ban liang, *meaning half* liang, *an ancient unit of weight. During Qin times the coinage used in previously existing states was replaced with circular coins like these.*

(Top) Head of a general denoted by double-tailed headgear, only worn by the highest ranking army personnel.

(Bottom) View of building spanning Pit Number Two where preliminary excavations have suggested that some 1,300 warriors, 450 horses and 89 chariots lie buried. (Far right bottom) Traces of a battle chariot remain in the mud that flooded the pits soon after their ransacking and flooding.

remind his subjects of the benefits he had brought them, for he had accounts of his achievements carved on steles and rocks on the summits of mountains. As his rule wore on, Qin Shihuangdi resorted to more extreme policies. When scholars dared to criticize him by invoking the model rulers of antiquity, Qin Shihuangdi, on the advice of Li Si, launched a sort of 'cultural revolution'. He ordered all works of literature and philosophy, including *The Book of History, The Book of Morals* and *The Book of Songs*, to be burnt. Even discussion of the contents of such classics became a crime. Eventually some 460 Confucian scholars were buried alive for their 'law-breaking'.

Such draconian measures made many enemies for the emperor. Three attempts were made on his life, but in 210BC he died naturally of illness while on an inspection tour. Li Si realized the importance of keeping the death a secret, returning to Xianyang and naming the new emperor before opponents could seize the opportunity to wrest power. The minister had the corpse concealed in the imperial chariot, and to disguise the putrid stench, he cleverly loaded a cart with salted fish to accompany the chariot back to the capital.

Qin Shihuangdi's dream that the House of Qin might rule the empire for countless generations proved a folly, for within just five years rebels stormed Xianyang and soon after, one of the rebel leaders, Liu Bang, established the Han Dynasty (206BC - AD220). Nevertheless, the First Emperor's corpse did make it back to the capital, to be entombed one year later (209BC) in the magnificent mausoleum under the guard of the terracotta army. And in this way Qin Shihuangdi did achieve the immortality and recognition he expected of what turned out to be a short-lived dynasty.

The Mausoleum

Construction work on Qin Shihuangdi's mausoleum began in the year he

became emperor, 246BC. It continued for about 40 years, even after his death in 210BC. Only the fall of the dynasty itself in 206BC halted work on the elaborate funerary complex.

The mausoleum is located at Lintong, facing Li Mountain in the south and the Wei River in the north. It measures approximately seven and a half kilometres square. Interior and exterior ramparts were built around its edge, probably out of the earth removed in the course of digging graves and chambers within the mausoleum.

The emperor's grave itself, *Qin Ling*, which lies

less than two kilometres west of the burial ground of the terracotta army, has not been excavated. It is a prominent mound resembling an upturned funnel. Beneath it is thought to lie the underground palace in which the remains of Qin Shihuangdi were laid to rest over 22 centuries ago. Preliminary archaeological investigations have revealed what appears to be the underground palace's wall just four metres below the surface.

What actually lies in the underground palace will remain a mystery for the moment, since the Chinese Ministry of Culture has no plans to excavate the site. In the meantime one must rely on references in *Records of the Historian*. The chronicler Sima Qian, who wrote his history of the period a century after the Qin Dynasty was overthrown, recorded that a labour force of 700,000 was used to construct the mausoleum. The underground palace was said to comprise various chambers, the most important being the burial chamber. It featured bronze walls with heaven and the known world — the Qin empire — being reproduced on the ceiling and floor respectively. The sun, moon and stars — the last represented by pearls — were depicted, while features on the floor included mechanically flowing rivers of mercury draining into a sea on which floated golden boats. Priceless treasures, live rare birds and animals were sealed inside while the emperor's body itself was enrobed in a funerary suit of gold and jade adorned with pearls. Qin Shihuangdi's childless wives were also buried alive with him.

(Top) Archaeologists at work in Pit Number One. All warriors found thus far were smashed by tomb looters or crushed when the tunnel structure they were housed in collapsed 22 centuries ago. Every warrior now standing upright is the result of painstaking reconstruction and renovation by a dedicated team of archaeologists.

Several ancillary graves have been found around that of the emperor. Some contained skeletons of horses while the occupants of others are almost certainly of royal lineage. Qin Shihuangdi fathered some 28 children and, after his death, they jostled bitterly for the succession. The direct heir, crown prince Fu Su, was killed by his younger brother Hu Hai, the second-in-line to the throne, who is also believed to have murdered many of his other brothers and sisters to secure his position. In all, some 17 skeletons, probably of princes and princesses, and perhaps of Qin Shihuangdi's parents, have been unearthed.

In the belief that the dead could enjoy all the luxuries of the living, prized treasures would have been buried with the emperor. Security against grave robbers was thus a major concern, and as a basic precaution, it was customary for those involved in the digging of royal tombs to be buried alive on completion of their work (See 'The Mystery of Pit Number Four', page 32). Whether any robbers actually dared to brave the loaded crossbows that were rumoured to lie in wait within the tomb's dark passageways is not known. Perhaps they still lie in wait — the answer to that mystery may be decades away.

The Terracotta Army

In the drought-stricken spring of March 1974, as peasants were digging a well to tap the groundwater beneath woods east of *Qin Ling*, they unearthed the head of the first terracotta warrior to see the light of day for more than 2,200 years.

Chinese archaeologists thought it likely that this accidental find would lead to the discovery of an army buried to guard Qin Shihuangdi in his afterlife. Two years' investigation confirmed those hopes, and an announcement was then made that the site probably contained 8,000 terracotta figures. The dig duly commenced, and 21 years later over 1,225 warriors and 88 horses have been unearthed from three pits. A fourth pit was found to be empty.

The positions of the pits, designated Pits One to Four according to their order of discovery, correspond to the prescribed military formation of a battle-ready army during Warring States and Qin times.

Infantry and Charioteers of Pit Number One

This is a rectangular pit measuring 230 metres in length from east to west and 62 metres in width from north to south. Extensive excavation in the eastern half of this pit has so far revealed 1,087 warriors, 32 horses and the traces of eight chariots.

The display consists of infantry and charioteers arranged in

A dismounted cavalryman and his horse, excavated from Pit Number Two. Cavalrymen wear simple headgear tied under their chins to prevent blowing off while riding. The hole on the horse's side was an essential design feature during the moulding and baking process to allow hot air to escape and prevent cracking of the mould. Warriors' torsos are also hollow.

battle formation. At the head, facing east, is the vanguard, consisting of three rows of 70 archers each. The south and north flanks are defended by troops facing outwards, some clothed in battle dress, others in armour and holding weapons, while more warriors on the west flank form the rearguard. In the centre of the formation the warriors are lined up in nine columns, and among them are interspersed impressions of eight wooden chariots, now decayed. Each chariot is drawn by four horses and would have borne a driver and two warriors.

Archaeologists have estimated that if completely excavated the pit would yield more than 6,000 warriors, 160 horses and 40 chariots.

Cavalry of Pit Number Two

This L-shaped pit lies just 20 metres north of Pit Number One. Whereas Pit Number One contains mainly infantry, Pit Number Two has a greater number of archers, chariots and cavalrymen leading their horses.

After an initial phase of 20 months' excavation and the removal of a great deal of earth and timbers, archaeologists have verified the shape of the pit. It was found to have 11 sloping entrances down which the terracotta warriors are believed to have been carted. Trial digging at several places unearthed 70 archers, some kneeling, others standing. They show more brilliant colour than those in the other pits. Some 52 horses were also discovered. There is evidence — including two shafts and a well between 50 and 100 years old — to suggest that locals may have stumbled across the terracotta warriors decades before the announced discovery.

Archaeologists say the military formation of Pit Number Two is far more complex than that in Pit Number One. The more numerous array of archers, chariots and cavalry suggests that in the battles of the day those troops in Pit Number Two would have been engaged in launching offensives and breaking up the enemy ranks. Once the enemy troops were on the run the cavalry would have given chase.

Excavations are only at a very early stage. Archaeologists think that the pit might hold a total of 1,300 figures, more than 450 horses and the traces of 89 battle chariots.

(Top) Bronze and stone equestrian implements. (Bottom) Terracotta horse head with reins and bit. (Following page) A standing archer excavated from Pit Number Two. This archer has no armour, only a simple robe, to allow freer movement and accurate marksmanship.

The Command Force of Pit Number Three

Though the smallest of the three pits, Pit Number Three is strategically the most important since the command of the entire terracotta army was stationed here. Excavation of this battle headquarters has revealed the traces of a chariot, four horses and 68 warriors. The four horses pulling the chariot and the four warriors behind it are in good condition, but many of the pit's other figures are headless or smashed completely. Numerous bronze weapons, and fragments of deer horn and animal bone have also been found. Animal sacrifice was probably part of the rites performed by commanders of a real army, who would have prayed to the gods for victory before a battle.

There is, however, one interesting omission. In Qin times, army commanders were normally issued with a special token of identification, a palm-sized tally which came in two equal halves. As the token was usually carved in the form of a tiger, it was called a 'tiger tally'. One half was held by the emperor, the other by the commander or general. To move troops, the general would have had to ask the emperor for permission. The emperor signified his agreement by giving his half of the tiger tally to the general. If the two halves fitted exactly, then all involved could be assured that the imperial order was genuine. No trace of a tiger tally, however, was found in Pit Number Three. This suggests that the commander of the terracotta army — which was above all an imperial guard — was probably in close attendance on the emperor himself.

Pit Construction and Destruction

All of the pits were tunnel structures built with clay and wood. None of them is particularly deep. The top of Pit Number Three, for example, is a little more than five metres below the ground surface. Once dug, the pit

(Preceding page) Detail of armour and twisted hand of a low ranking warrior. (Top) Side view of a general's head. (Bottom) Rebuilt wooden structure in Pit Number One.

(Top) Heads of horses and a warrior's torso in a partly-excavated state. (Bottom) Bronze hinged mechanism from a crossbow. (Following page) Archers, denoted by their absence of armour to allow freedom of movement, form the vanguard in Pit Number One.

floors were levelled and paved with bricks, which have been well preserved. The pits' walls were lined with wood and sizeable roof beams were laid down and held up with the aid of timber supports. Curved impressions made by these heavy beams can be seen on the divisions between the passageways in Pit Number One. The distance from the pit floor to the roof was 3.2 metres.

Next began the sealing-up process. To prevent the infiltration of water, the wooden roofs were covered in reed matting onto which impervious clay was tamped. At this stage workmen would have carted in and positioned the thousands of terracotta warriors which range in height from 1.80 to 2.02 metres (kneeling warriors are approximately 1.2 metres high) and weigh approximately 150 kilograms. With the 8,000-man army in battle-ready position, the wooden doors were emplaced and also sealed with clay. The closed, underground barracks was now in complete darkness.

But not for long. Despite the meticulous planning for Qin Shihuangdi's afterlife, his underground fortress remained undisturbed for a mere five years. As his sons struggled to succeed him, discontented peasants rebelled. A warlord from the former Kingdom of Chu, Xiang Yu, eventually stormed Xianyang, the Qin capital, and shortly after the terracotta army did indeed face the atrocities of war when Xiang Yu's peasant rebels entered the mausoleum.

They probably carted off all that was precious and moveable. As

for the pits, they might have remained intact but for the fact that the roofs on some had probably already collapsed. This was certainly caused by rainwater draining inside and rotting the wooden beams. Looters were therefore able to enter the pits. The terracotta warriors themselves were thought not to be worth removing, and were in any case too big and cumbersome. Nevertheless, most were smashed. The ransackers carried away instead valuable bronze weapons. Beams blackened with charcoal indicate that fires were started in the pits, but the warriors were only damaged, not destroyed. The fire did, however, burn off nearly all their paint and caused the collapse of the tunnel structures, though ironically that buried the army safely for the next 22 centuries.

Over two millennia later, the pits do indeed resemble battlefields. After painstaking archaeological work, many warriors now stand upright, while others lied beheaded and dismembered on the ground.

(Preceding page) A general, 2.02 metres in height, excavated from Pit Number Two. Generals are the tallest and heaviest members of the army. This one highlights the skill of the artisan who made him: he exhibits advanced age denoting military experience, and appears calm in command of his men. (Top) Hand of a general with long, ruffled sleeves. The bronze sword he once held was probably looted. (Left top) Armour on the shoulder of a warrior. (Left middle) Footwear of warriors including (right) treaded sole of a kneeling archer. (Left bottom) Rear view of a middle-ranking warrior's head.

Warrior Sculpture

Every figurine is different. Such individuality has prompted speculation that they were modelled on real personalities in Qin Shihuangdi's army. One can discern from their facial features and apparel differences of age, function and rank. Sometimes it is even possible to speculate about their character and temperament. However, collectively the figures do exhibit some general racial characteristics: they have squarish faces, wide foreheads, thick lips, moustaches and beards. The majority have alert expressions and a steely gaze.

The figures are all quite tall, with generals and commanders being the tallest and most portly. Apart from their greater size, generals can be clearly identified by their double-tailed headgear, longer tunics falling to below the knee, and minimal fish-scale pattern armour on the midriff which hangs in an inverted V-shape a little below the waist. On the chest and neck they have bow-like decorations, while

their feet are shod in boots with upturned toes. The sleeves of generals' tunics are usually long enough partly to cover the hands, since generals directed their troops and rarely engaged in direct combat themselves.

Officers have simpler headgear and usually wear a little more armour, sometimes on the shoulders, but not on the chest. Boots are flat-toed and box-shaped. Sleeves leave the

hands clear and free, for the officer both directs his troops and may need to lead them by example into combat.

Cavalrymen are found dismounted in front of their terracotta horses. They can be recognized by their sleeveless jackets of armour, which appears thick, and is composed of quite large, squarish plates which seem to be 'riveted' together. Headgear is extremely simple and close-fitting and is secured with a chin strap to prevent it blowing off while riding. Shoes are the lightest and smallest of all those worn by the army.

Archers are portrayed in active, vigilant and carrying postures. The active ones usually wear simple battle robes with no armour, and their arms are in the process of drawing back their bows. Kneeling archers are more plentiful. They are crouched down on one knee in readiness for combat and they wear quite heavy armour on both their torsos and shoulders. Viewed from the rear their boots can be seen to have a distinct tread. But the bulk of the army's archers, in Pit Number One, are standing at ease.

The infantry wear either battle robes or bulkier armour. Their hair is usually tied into topknots and their hands are poised to carry spears. The charioteers are in more active poses. They have both arms stretched out slightly so as to hold the reins to drive their vehicles. Their horses, approximately 1.72 metres in height and slightly over 2 metres in length, look sturdy with big, bright, alert eyes, wide-open nostrils and impressive muscularity.

Moulding and Painting of the Figures

The warriors are composed of baked clay that was made by mixing loess with quartz sand. Anatomical parts — the heads, ears, torsos, arms, hands, legs and feet — were moulded separately. Individual adornments such as hats, hair, tunics, armour and gaiters were then moulded onto completed bodies from sheets of clay. At this stage the art of the craftsmen came into play as individual characteristics were produced, or perhaps copied. Some of the more delightful fine personal touches include the furrows on a general's forehead and the smile of a young warrior.

After the warriors had dried naturally in the shade they were placed in

(Preceding page) Head of a standing archer excavated from Pit Number Two. (Left top) Goose-shaped belt hook and (Left bottom) belt hook showing a man charging with a spear. (Bottom left) A warrior's head which still exhibits some glaze and pigmentation. The warriors were painted, but most of their colour was burnt off in fires started by tomb looters soon after the emperor's entombment. (Bottom right) Rear view of kneeling archer. (Following page) A commander in a plain gown. The absence of armour suggests the commander's superior role, directing troops rather than engaging in combat. Nevertheless, this warrior's right hand is poised to hold a spear.

furnaces at temperatures of 950-1050 degrees Centigrade. Once baked, they were painted in a variety of colours including green, red, purplish-red, flesh, purple, blue and white.

Craftsmen in the workshops were obliged to etch their names on the figures. In this way those producing substandard work could be identified. To date, 87 different family names have been found etched on the warriors, usually on the back of their belts.

Weapons

An arsenal of weaponry has been found in the pits: they are actual armaments used in warfare during the Qin Dynasty. They fall into three categories: daggers and swords used in close combat; long-handled arms such as spears and axes; and bows and arrows, and crossbows.

Weapons were made of bronze and copper alloys according to the demands of the particular armament. Among them, the long bronze sword draws particular attention. As slender as a willow leaf, it measures 90 centimetres in length and still possesses a keen cutting edge. It is thinner and longer than swords made in the Warring States period, and gives the swordsman greater thrusting power. Such bronze swords underwent the first rust-proofing in history with the application of chromium oxide coatings. Today, the swords are still rust-free, and they exhibit a bluish-grey shining lustre.

Bronze Chariots and Horses

In August 1978, archaeologists unearthed a small gold ornament as they made a test drilling to the west of *Qin Ling*. Two years later in December 1980, two chariots, each with two spoked wheels and drawn by four horses, were unearthed — totally smashed, apart from the solid bronze steeds and charioteers.

These wonders of metalworking are about half the actual size of chariots used by Emperor Qin Shihuangdi on his inspection tours of the empire. Qin Dynasty chariot construction won great admiration even from two of the state's greatest adversaries, Xiang Yu and Liu Bang, who also envied the grandeur and prowess of Qin charioteers.

The two bronze chariots were certainly crafted specifically for Qin Shihuangdi's afterlife. Since excavation they have been successfully pieced together. The larger of the two, the *an che*, is 3.17 metres in length, weighs about 1,200 kilograms and is made of bronze, gold and silver components — about 3,462

(Top) Bronze arrowheads, photographed in situ as found by excavators. (Bottom left) Hollow, bronze cudgel ends for mounting on poles. Triangular in shape at their apex, these weapons were used in close combat in either thrusting or beating fashion. (Bottom right) Bronze spearhead engraved with characters si gong (someone's name)

separate metallic parts in all. It has a closed carriage with small, rhombus-shaped lattice windows on three sides for ventilation, and a door at the back. The domed roof is of very thin bronze sheeting laid over a frame of 36 bow-shaped spokes (corresponding to the number of districts in the Qin Empire) which are about 6 millimetres in diameter. It covers the passenger carriage and the seated charioteer, which is also made of solid bronze. Special design features include small windows for privacy and ventilation, interior decoration with cloud, dragon and phoenix patterns, and probably cushioning and quilting for a comfortable ride — traces of silk were found.

The second chariot, the *gao che*, which was found in front of the other, is a vanguard vehicle with no covered compartment. At 2.25 metres in length and weighing 1,061 kilograms, it is smaller and lighter than the *an che*, but it has the same number of horses. With its greater power to weight ratio this was a swifter vehicle and would have run ahead of the *an che* as an escort. Its canopy is higher, allowing the charioteer to stand upright and gain a good view of the road ahead.

Both chariots exhibit surprising levels of the ancients' metallurgical skills, metal-shaping technology and artistry. Temperature controls and casting methods of the time were clearly advanced and ingenious. For example, the flexibility of leather halters and reins was reproduced in metal by fitting together some 84 one-centimetre-long tubes. It is just another of

(Top) Head of a cavalryman showing simple headgear affixed by a chin strap. (Bottom) Three terracotta horses that once pulled a battle chariot, the wooden parts of which have since decayed. (Following page) Charioteer, 1.90 metres in height, excavated from Pit Number One. (Pages 30-31) Rear view of column of infantrymen in Pit Number One. At bottom left the impressions left by roof beams of the original tunnel structure can be seen.

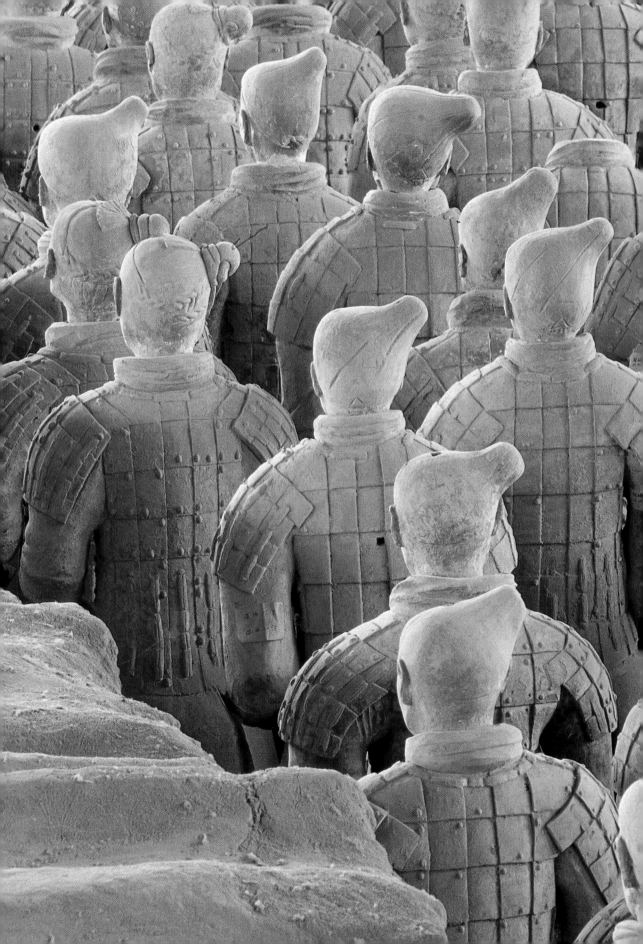

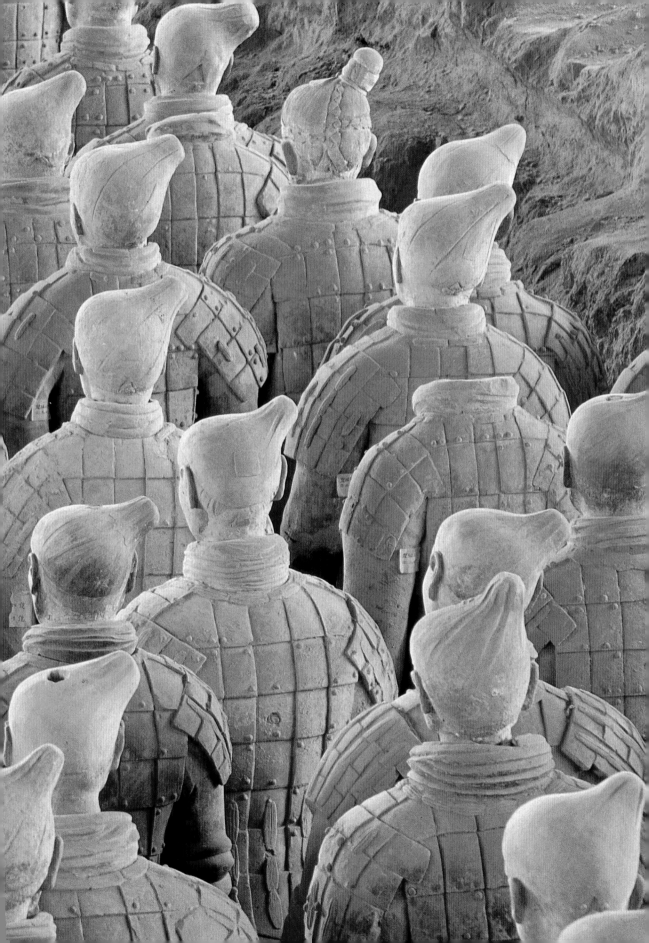

(Top) Topknot of a low ranking warrior. Higher ranking warriors wear some form of headgear. (Bottom) A commander found standing behind a chariot, excavated from Pit Number One.

the countless, astonishing details revealed by treasures excavated from the vast mausoleum of Emperor Qin Shihuangdi. In the future more wonderful discoveries are sure to be made in the precincts of the afterlife realm of China's first emperor.

THE MYSTERY OF PIT NUMBER FOUR

The euphoria which greeted the discovery of yet another pit — a fourth — turned out to be premature when in 1995 a re-excavation found the pit to be totally empty. Situated between the other three pits, the fourth pit measures 48 metres in width and 96 metres in length. And like the others it was at about the same depth, 4.8 metres.

What was the pit dug for? What was put inside, if anything? Was it robbed? These questions have puzzled archaeologists, but Yuan Zhongyi, director of the Museum of Terracotta Warriors and Horses of Emperor Qin Shihuangdi, has revealed the likely answer.

Yuan Zhongyi notes that standard military formations of the time were usually made up of central forces with left and right flanks. Pit Number One represents the right flank, Pit Two the left flank, and Pit Three the command headquarters. So where is the central force in the army? Pit Number Four could be the answer. But it is empty. Why?

The answer is hinted at in Sima Qian's *Records of the Historian*. The chronicler of the times wrote that Emperor Qin Shihuangdi had accepted a suggestion from one of his ministers to pardon those criminals who had built his mausoleum. In fact they were probably needed in the army to quell the peasant uprisings that burst out around the time of the emperor's death. Hence the pit earmarked for the live burial of men remained empty. Funerary practices for royals during the Warring States period, which immediately preceded the Qin Dynasty, included the burial of actual living soldiers, not clay figurines, to act as tomb guards. It seems that Qin Shihuangdi planned to have both, but secular needs called loudest: the defence of the empire was at stake.

Pit Number Four has now been filled in again, except for its very northwestern corner. There one can peep into the dark grave from which thousands of men were spared.

A CHRONOLOGY OF PERIODS IN CHINESE HISTORY

Palaeolithic	c.600,000 – 7000 BC
Neolithic	c.7000 – 1600 BC
Shang	c.1600 – 1027 BC
Western Zhou	1027 – 771 BC
Eastern Zhou	770 – 256 BC
Spring and Autumn Annals	770 – 476 BC
Warring States	475 – 221 BC
Qin	221 – 206 BC
Western (Former) Han	206 BC – 8 AD
Xin	9 – 24
Eastern (Later) Han	25 – 220
Three Kingdoms	220 – 265
Western Jin	265 – 316
Northern and Southern Dynasties	317 – 589
Sixteen Kingdoms	317 – 439
Former Zhao	304 – 329
Former Qin	351 – 383
Later Qin	384 – 417
Northern Wei	386 – 534
Western Wei	535 – 556
Northern Zhou	557 – 581
Sui	581 – 618
Tang	618 – 907
Five Dynasties	907 – 960
Liao	916 – 1125
Northern Song	960 – 1127
Southern Song	1127 – 1279
Jin (Jurchen)	1115 – 1234
Yuan (Mongol)	1279 – 1368
Ming	1368 – 1644
Qing (Manchu)	1644 – 1911
Republic of China	1911 – 1949
People's Republic of China	1949 –

Author of the text, **William Lindesay**, lived in Xi'an for four years, during which time he visited the mausoleum of Qin Shihuangdi on 15 occasions. His previous books include *Alone on the Great Wall* (Hodder & Stoughton, London 1989) and *The Great Wall* (Pacific Century Publishers, Hong Kong, 1997), the latter in the same Close Up series as this title.

Lindesay based his writing on an archaeological text provided by **Guo Baofa**, director of the Preservation and Conservation Department, Museum of Terracotta Warriors and Horses of Qin Shihuangdi. Guo studied archaeology at Beijing University, and his papers include *Seals of the Qin and Han Dynasties* and *Qin Military Formations and War Strategies*.